EASTER CRAFTS

ANNALEES LIM

First published in 2014 by Wayland
Copyright © Wayland 2014

Wayland
338 Euston Road
London NW1 3BH

Wayland Australia
Hachette Children's Books
Level 17/207
Kent Street
Sydney, NSW 2000

Editor: Elizabeth Brent
Craft stylist: Annalees Lim
Designer: Dynamo Ltd
Photographer: Simon Pask, N1 Studios

The website addresses (URLs) and QR codes included in this book were valid at the time of going to press. However, it is possible that contents or addresses may have changed since the publication of this book. No responsibility for any such changes can be accepted by either the author or the Publisher.

ISBN   978 0 7502 8194 2
eBook ISBN   978 0 7502 8700 5

Dewey number: 745.5'941667-dc23

Printed in China

10 9 8 7 6 5 4 3 2 1

Wayland is a division of Hachette Children's Books,
an Hachette UK company.

www.hachette.co.uk

Picture acknowledgements:
All step-by-step craft photography: Simon Pask, N1 Studios;
images used throughout for creative graphics: Shutterstock

Contents

Easter

Easter is a celebration of new life and re-birth, and people celebrate this holiday in many different ways. In this book you will find simple crafts to help make your Easter festivities really fun. Each project will take you only about 10 minutes to make, so you will still have plenty of time to go in search of tasty treats on an Easter egg hunt!

Bunny Egg Cup: pages 18-19

All of these projects use different papers, from tissue paper to card, and paper plates. Before you go out and buy supplies, have a look at what you have at home. There are lots of things that can be recycled, such as old Easter cards, which are great for cutting out flowers to decorate the Easter bunny picture on pages 14–15, sweetie wrappers and foils to use as decorations, leftover ribbons from packaging, or old envelopes to use as scrap paper. Whatever you find, store it away in a craft bag or box, ready for the next time you get creative.

Crafting can be messy, especially if you are using glitter or glues, so make sure you cover all your work surfaces with old newspaper or a plastic tablecloth before you begin. Always wash your hands after you have used glue to stop your works of art being ruined by sticky fingers, and always ask an adult to help you with scissors or sharp compasses.

Crêpe paper chicken hanging: pages 22-23

Easter basket: pages 8-9

So with Easter fast approaching, take some time to get messy with these makes to decorate and celebrate this time of year.

Flower bonnet

Parade around with pride in this beautiful bonnet, which is covered in delicate daffodils.

1

Measure around your head using the tape measure, then cut a piece of green card the same length, and 10cm wide. You may have to staple two lengths of card together.

2

Cut triangle shapes out of the top to make it look like grass, and then staple the ends together to make a headband.

Watch this step-by-step video of the flower bonnet being made!

3

Fold one of the cake cases into quarters and round off the top. Open it up and it will make four petals. Glue on some rolled-up orange tissue paper to make the centre of the flower.

4

Make five daffodils and glue them onto the green headband.

5

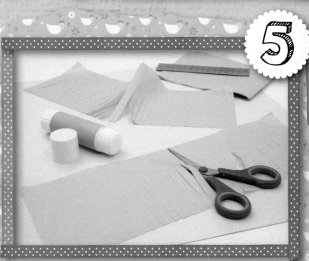

Cut a 10cm-wide piece of tissue paper to the same length as your headband. Cut slits into the top and glue it to the inside of the headband so the cut bits stick out over the top.

There are lots of other plants that are in flower around Easter, so step outside to get inspiration for your bonnet. Use different-coloured cake cases to create different sorts of flowers.

Easter basket

Make this colourful Easter-egg-shaped basket to collect all your chocolatey treats in when you are on an egg hunt.

You will need:

- Two coloured paper, thin plastic or polystyrene bowls
- Scissors
- A stapler
- Yellow card
- A ruler
- Ribbon
- Craft glue
- Sticky dots

1

Cut out some triangles from one side of each bowl to make it look like a cracked egg.

2

Put the two bowls together and staple around the edge to make the main basket shape.

3 Cut out a 3cm x 30cm strip from the yellow card and staple it onto the basket to make a handle.

4 Make two bows from the ribbon and glue them onto the handle to cover the staples.

5 Stick lots of colourful sticky dots all over the basket.

Make more baskets from white paper bowls and staple some card ears onto the top to turn them into bunnies! Remember to draw a face on the front. You could even stick a white pom-pom tail to the back too.

Folded flowers

These pretty flowers make lovely Easter decorations. You could scatter them around the centre of a table to brighten up your Easter Sunday meal, or hang them from the ceiling as a mobile.

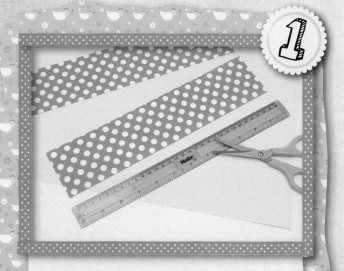

1

Cut two pieces of patterned paper into a rectangle that measures 7cm x 30cm.

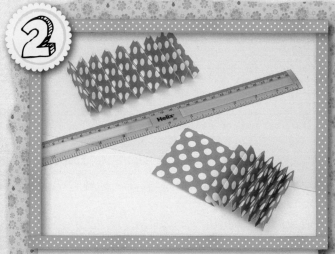

2

Fold each of the papers into a concertina, with each fold 1cm deep.

3

Round off the top of both concertinas.

4

Unfold the concertinas and staple them both together into a circle shape.

5

Cut out a circle of card to make the middle of the flower and glue it in place.

Stick the flowers to the end of green garden sticks to make them into a bunch of flowers. They will look great in a vase and will brighten any room.

Felt chick card

People will love receiving this Easter card. It feels furry and feathery, like a real chick.

You will need:

- A4 blue card
- A protractor
- A pencil
- Scissors
- Yellow, black and white felt
- Craft glue
- Yellow feathers
- Orange paper

Fold the blue card in half, and then fold one of the halves in half again.

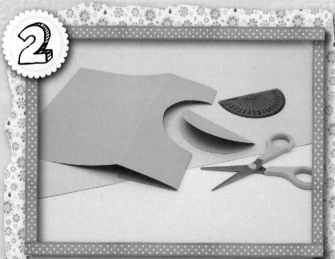

Draw a small semicircle onto the second folded section, and cut it out to make a circle.

Watch this step-by-step video of the felt chick card being made!

12

3

Cut out a piece of yellow felt that is slightly bigger than the circle and stick it to the back of the circle-shaped hole using some craft glue.

4

Make some eyes from the black and white felt and stick them onto the body, then use more craft glue to stick yellow feathers to either side of the felt circle.

5

Cut out a triangle beak and some feet from the orange paper and stick them onto the card.

Use different colours of felt to turn your cards into other animals, such as sheep or bunnies.

13

Easter bunny picture

Make the cute Easter bunnies bounce and skip over the hills in this fun spinning picture.

You will need:

- A plate
- A pencil
- Green card
- Blue card
- Scissors
- White and yellow paper
- A glue stick
- A black felt-tipped pen
- A pink crayon or pencil
- Paper fasteners

1

Draw around the plate onto the green and blue card and cut out the shapes so you have two circles that are identical in size.

2

Cut a wavy line off the top of the green circle.

14

3 Cut six bunny shapes out of the white paper and stick them onto the edge of the blue circle.

4 Go round the bunny shapes in black pen. Draw ears, legs and a tail onto each bunny shape and colour the ears in pink too.

5 Place the green circle on top of the blue circle and press a paper fastener into the middle to hold them together. Decorate the green hills with yellow paper flowers.

Spin the blue circle to make it look as if the bunnies are bouncing over the hills. You could also make a spinning picture to show sheep leaping over a flowery meadow or birds flying through the sky.

Seasonal sparkling mobile

Easter happens at about the same time every year but you never know what the weather will be like. Make this raindrop mobile to hang inside to keep the rain away outside.

You will need:
- A4 white card
- A black felt-tipped pen
- Scissors
- A hole punch
- Silver thread
- A ruler
- Cotton wool balls
- A glue stick
- Silver card

1

Fold the white card in half, and draw a cloud shape on one side. Cut this out, and make one hole at the top and five holes at the bottom using the hole punch.

2

Tie a loop of silver thread to the top of the cloud and five 30cm pieces of thread to the bottom of the cloud.

3

Glue balls of cotton wool onto the front and back of the cloud using the glue stick.

4

Cut out 26 matching raindrop shapes from the silver card.

5

Glue a pair of raindrops around a silver thread. Repeat until you have glued all of the raindrops onto all five threads.

You can add more things to your mobile. Try grey storm clouds, a rainbow or even a pair of shiny wellington boots.

Bunny egg cup

Make this cute bunny decoration to show off your chocolate treats. They will look so good, you won't be able to resist eating them for long!

You will need:

- A foil-wrapped Easter egg
- An old egg cup
- White card
- A ruler
- Scissors
- Pink card
- A glue stick
- Googly eyes
- A black felt-tipped pen
- Blu-Tack

1

Make a headband for the egg using a small, 1cm-wide strip of card. Stick two bunny ears, made of white card and pink card, to the top of the band.

2

Stick two googly eyes onto the headband.

3

Cut out a heart shape from the pink card and draw a nose onto it. Cut out some white teeth and stick them to the back of the heart.

4

Glue the nose and teeth onto the headband.

5

Make two sets of paws out of the white card. Tuck the front paws into the egg cup and use Blu-Tack to stick the back paws onto the base of the egg cup.

Ask an adult to help you remove the inside of a real egg. Do this by making two small holes in the shell, and blowing out the contents. Then you can paint the eggshell and it will last year after year.

Easter egg pin badge

This clay badge is great to wear during the Easter celebrations. It is so simple to make that you will want to make one for all your friends and family too.

You will need:
- Coloured polymer clay
- A rolling pin
- A blunt knife or clay tools
- A brooch pin

1

Roll out some clay so that it is 0.5 cm thick.

2

Make small balls of clay in different colours and press them into the flat piece of clay using the rolling pin.

3

Using the clay tools or knife, cut out an egg shape, making sure you smooth down the edges.

4

Press a brooch pin into the back of the clay egg.

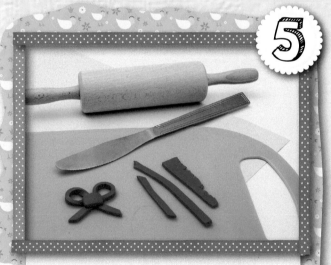

5

Make a clay bow and press it onto the middle of the egg. Bake the clay as instructed on the packet so that it goes hard and is ready to wear.

Pin the badge to the front of a folded piece of card to make an Easter card that doubles up as a gift!

Crêpe paper chicken hanging

These clucking chickens will hang anywhere, but if you put them near an open window you will see their feathers rustle in the wind!

1 Make two feet from the orange card and sandwich them in between a folded paper plate. Glue the plate down to stick them firmly into place.

2 Cut a wavy shape out of red card to make the chicken's comb. Glue this to the folded edge of the paper plate.

3

Cut two wing shapes out of yellow card.

4

Fold a length of yellow crêpe paper into a loose concertina and cut a 'v' from the bottom. When you open this out it will look like feathers. Tape rows of these feathers to the chicken's body.

5

Stick the wings onto the body and make an orange beak to go underneath the comb. Finally glue on some googly eyes and staple a strip of green crêpe paper to the top so your chicken can hang up.

Make some chicks in the same way but use smaller paper plates instead. Remember chicks don't have a comb, so you won't need to make this.

Glossary

bonnet a type of hat, often decorated with flowers

comb the wavy crest on the head of a chicken

confetti tiny pieces of coloured paper

feathery covered in feathers

festivities festive activities, or celebrations

meadow a field of grass, often used to graze animals on

recycle to re-make something into something else

skip to move along with light, hopping steps

Index

24

10 minute CRAFTS

Titles in the series:

SPRING
978 0 7502 8403 5

Fluffy sheep, Life of a seed, Leaf print flowers, Daffodil paperweight, Bark rubbing, Bouncing bunnies, Twig hanging, Potted flowers, Soil picture

EASTER
978 0 7502 8194 2

Flower bonnet, Easter basket, Folded flowers, Felt chick card, Easter bunny picture, Seasonal sparkling hanging, Bunny egg cup, Easter egg pin badge, Crêpe-paper chicken hanging

SUMMER
978 0 7502 8330 4

Crawling crabs, Butterfly pegs, Seascape in a bottle, Sandcastles, Flower prints, Mini kites, Sunflower pot, Rafts, Starfish

MOTHER'S AND FATHER'S DAY
978 0 7502 8196 6

Stripy wool-covered pot, Pop-up card, Glasses case, Trinket box, Fancy tea bag jar, Mouse mouse-mat, You're #1 mug, Lolly stick photo frame, Photo keyring

AUTUMN
978 0 7502 8329 8

Pine cone squirrel, Apple hedgehog prints, Dried leaf bonfire, Field mouse, Spider web, Mini owls, Scarecrow, Book worm, Conker creatures

HALLOWEEN
978 0 7502 8195 9

Zombie finger puppet, Witch's broomstick, Pumpkin patch, RIP VIP invitation, Paper plate mummy hanging, Spooky sweetie tree, Bat hanging, Skeleton torch projection, Black cat lantern

WINTER
978 0 7502 8351 9

Mini pine forest, Bird bingo, Twirling twig hanging, Bird feeder, Sticks and stones, Scented hanging, Ice mobile, Potato print snowman, Penguin skittles

CHRISTMAS
978 0 7502 8172 0

Felt stocking, Sleigh sweetie dish, Paper ribbon wreath, Toilet roll tube reindeer, Pine cone elf Santa tree decoration, Candy cane Christmas card, Christmas tree advent calendar, Rocking robin bauble